At the Cross

CWR

Abby Guinness

Contents

Introduction

The death and resurrection of Jesus are the 'crux' of the Christian faith and our theology. To those of us who believe, they are the crux of all creation and eternity. As the apostle Paul says in 1 Corinthians 15:14: 'if Christ has not been raised, our preaching is useless and so is your faith' (NIV).

It all happened in just a few days, a couple of thousand years ago. We specifically remember and mark these incredible events during one weekend every year. But what would happen if we sat with the crucifixion for longer, as if we were able to hold it in our hands, and turn it around to look at it from different perspectives; different angles? Lent gives us an opportunity to focus on the events of those few days and consider their impact more widely. It may be that for these sessions, and the times in between, you want to find a holding cross or something similar – it could represent the focus you will give to the events of The Passion narrative as you revisit it in your mind.

Together, in these sessions, we'll spend some time thinking about six people who witnessed the crucifixion. They were real people with thoughts, experiences and responses like ours. My background is in theatre and I have a love of thinking about things dramatically. I naturally consider human nature and personal stories to help me understand and explore the Scriptures. I would love it if you would enter into that with me. There is a short monologue in each session alongside other thoughts, ideas and discussion points. They form the basis of each study and I pray they will help you find fresh perspective on your own interpretation of the biblical text.

The theologian N.T. Wright speaks a lot about using our imagination to expand our understanding of God's world. He encourages us to see that, 'the Bible is there to rekindle our imagination so that we can worship God for all he's worth.' Of course our imaginations can be inaccurate or unreliable, but we are reassured that 'the Bible gives us the framework within which we can start to imagine Christianly.'[1]

Conversely, our imagination may be helped by knowledge that can guide it in to new places. When exploring biblical texts, I have found it useful to study some Bible commentaries and history to help expand the places that my imagination can reach with confidence. Much of this research has been done on the internet, which now provides endless resources (but do be careful to check the validity of the source). I recommend www.scripture4all.org for an 'interlinear' Bible that gives the literal translations from Greek and Hebrew alongside the King James Version so we can see the development of the text.

The combination of using both our mind and our heart, along with the inspiration of the Holy Spirit, is the 'sweet spot' where we may hear new things from God. I encourage you to be open to the Holy Spirit during this study. He inspired the writing of Scripture, and should also be invited to inspire our reading and study of it.

The crucifixion, though central to our faith, is not an easy thing to spend an extended time contemplating. I recently watched the film *The Passion of the Christ* [2] for the second time and found myself (again) cowering from the screen. The depiction of such extreme human suffering, coupled with my belief that it was experienced to secure my own life and freedom, was overwhelming. It may be a worthy reminder of the cost of my salvation but, honestly, it is easier to censor or avoid much of the time. So it is worth my mentioning right at the start that although we will spend time exploring the crucifixion specifically, we do so knowing that the resurrection is fully integrated into its narrative. The benefit for us is that we know what happened next and we respond in light of the whole picture – at least, what we have seen of it so far.

Those present at the event of the crucifixion did not all fully realise what was to come just days later, even though the Old Testament and Jesus' teaching had been pointing towards it. As we study these characters over the coming weeks, it is interesting to consider their viewpoint and how our own may differ. For us, everything we consider is in the light of the resurrection (and the rest of the New Testament). That gives us a wider context for consideration, as well as the knowledge of the coming return of Jesus.

My prayer is that you may meet with Jesus through these studies, and that you may be enabled to know Him in a new or different way. Our focus on the people who witnessed the crucifixion will ripple out into a wider recognition of the relationships Jesus had on earth. I hope these characters will inspire and deepen our friendship with Jesus and motivate us to bring others to know Him too.

[1] Both quotes from N.T. Wright, 'The Bible and Christian Imagination', transcript of N.T. Wright's lecture at Seattle Pacific University, 18 May, 2005. Found at www.spu.edu/depts/uc/response/summer2k5/features/imagination.asp (accessed June 2016).

[2] *The Passion of the Christ.* Dir. Mel Gibson. USA: Icon Productions, 2004.

The Centurion: Finding Truth

Mark 15:33-39

Icebreaker

Take it in turns to tell the group two things about yourself – one should be true and one made up. The others must see if they can guess which is true, and you must own up if they're right!

Opening Prayer

Truthful Father, thank You that nothing is hidden from You.
Truthful Jesus, sorry for the times we miss the truth or lie.
Truthful Spirit, help us to discern what is right.
Please reveal Your truth to us. Amen.

Setting the Scene

Each of the Gospels has its own identity – each reveals certain things that its writer is particularly concerned with.

John's Gospel is littered with references to the truth, and helps us understand that Jesus *is* the truth and the Spirit guides us towards Him.

'Jesus answered, "I am the way and the truth and the life. No one comes to the Father except through me"' (John 14:6, NIV).

Mark's is the shortest Gospel. He is concise. I like to think of him as a 'no nonsense' writer. I can imagine him saying, 'Let's get to the point here – what people really need to know is the truth that Jesus is the Son of God.'

This truth is for everyone and all of the Gospels tell stories of those who begin to understand it. Jesus tells us it is worth seeking. 'And you will know the truth, and the truth will make you free' (John 8:32).

What we see in today's passage from Mark is a person unexpectedly discovering the surprising truth of Jesus' identity.

The soldiers at the crucifixion are working for the Roman Empire. They are Gentiles; non-Jews. They might therefore be considered 'the enemy' by the Jewish people. They oversee and administer punishments and executions regularly. Perhaps they are hardened to suffering. Would they even care whether someone in their charge deserves to die? They must get on with their job or be punished themselves. In this case, because the Jewish leaders want this 'heretic', Jesus, crucified, the soldiers are providing a service that pleases many of the Jewish elite.

The darkness that falls as Jesus dies represents the spiritual blindness of the Jews. They miss the truth of who He is, in direct contrast with the only one present who has not *chosen* to watch. The soldier finds the truth through the darkness.

Bible Reading

Mark 15:33–39

'When it was noon, darkness came over the whole land until three in the afternoon. At three o'clock Jesus cried out with a loud voice, *"Eloi, Eloi, lema sabachthani?"* which means, "My God, my God, why have you forsaken me?" When some of the bystanders heard it, they said, "Listen, he is calling for Elijah." And someone ran, filled a sponge with sour wine, put it on a stick, and gave it to him to drink, saying, "Wait, let us see whether Elijah will come to take him down." Then Jesus gave a loud cry and breathed his last. And the curtain of the temple was torn in two, from top to bottom. Now when the centurion, who stood facing him, saw that in this way he breathed his last, he said, "Truly this man was God's Son!"'

Session Focus

The soldier at the cross – an imagined inner monologue

I've never seen dark like that in the day. People think of Golgotha as dark. I admit it can get dark in a storm, but not like that. Anyway, no rain or clouds, just pitch black for three hours when it should've been broad daylight. Maybe God couldn't bear to watch.

I watched. The poor guy yelled as if to someone miles away – asked God why he'd gone and left him so alone.

I think we all felt alone in those hours, couldn't see far enough to feel a friend. The daylight's back now but it still feels cold.

They never finish that loud. Not usually that quick either. Normal way is slow suffocation and no breath left to croak. It was like this one chose to go. Made some kind of statement and wanted everyone to know.

And when he did it, the earth shook. I don't know if it was fear or rage, but I tell you straight – it was shaking. There were breaking rocks and groans underground.

I've done this a fair few times. It's a job. But it never felt like this. I'm not scared. I don't get scared. Alright. Maybe a bit. What's bothering me? Big, hairy, scary me? This one's rattled me.

Some deserve it, some don't. I like to try and figure out which. Check for the evidence in how they take it. Check on the faces of whoever turns up. Looking around these faces I can't get a consensus.

Loss of a hero.

Chuffed at just desserts.

Intrigued.

Surprised.

Confused.

Unsure.

No two faces the same. But I think I know.

Surely there was something in the rumours. Surely there was something beyond him. This man was the son of God.

And I just watched him die.

The passage starts with the unusual fall of darkness. Some astronomers calculate an eclipse at this time and it fulfils prophecies from the Old Testament (Amos 8:9 and Jer. 15:9). This is the moment when the one described as, 'light ... coming into the world' (John 1:9, NIV), is extinguished.

When Jesus cries out, it's believed to be a Syriac dialect. *Eloi* means 'God', whereas the name for Elijah was *Elias*. Some of the bystanders jump on the similarity to claim Jesus is calling on Elijah rather than on God – an insult to suggest that a Jew would call on a prophet instead of the Lord.

Many theologians calculate the hour of Jesus' death as being the time of the Passover evening sacrifice. The sacrificed lamb on this day represented God's deliverance of the Israelites from death – the lamb's blood on the doorposts signalled to the angel of death to 'pass over' their households on the night they gained their freedom. Jesus' death and resurrection achieve the ultimate deliverance from death and passage to freedom. The priests and leaders should have been present at the sacrificial ceremony. Instead, they were desperate to watch and confirm the death of this troublesome heretic, not understanding its significance.

Matthew Henry's seminal commentary[i] claims that the loud shout before Jesus' death tells us a lot. It was unusual for anyone dying on a cross to have the strength to shout in this moment, but instead of slipping away from life with no resistance, Jesus went by choice, shouting defeat to sin, death, His enemies and the darkness.

The soldier doesn't see the tearing of the Temple veil, but we are given this important piece of accompanying information. The curtain hung between the holy place, and the *most* holy place. Only one priest at a time, chosen by drawn lots, was allowed in the most holy place to burn incense to God. Jesus' death opens access to the Holy of Holies; it breaks the divide between those who are sanctified and those who are not; it opens heaven to all who believe.

Access for everyone includes access for the Roman Gentile soldier. Why him? Perhaps to demonstrate that no one is too hardened to receive Christ. No one can be on the 'wrong' side. Jesus makes Himself known to all, even to those who persecute Him. It is also interesting that this centurion is willing to make a public declaration of his belief, when the disciples seem unable to do so throughout this time (see Peter's denial in Mark 14).

❓ Discussion Starters

1. What kind of things do you think of as creating 'spiritual darkness' in our society today? Do they obscure truth? How?

_____

_____

_____

_____

_____

2. Are there some people you would consider more difficult for Jesus to reach? What things might help or hinder their discovery of His true identity?

_____

_____

_____

_____

_____

3. For you, how important is it to know the truth? How far would you go to find it?

_____

_____

_____

_____

_____

4. If you have, how did you decide that the story of Jesus' death and resurrection was true? Are there parts of the story you struggle with?

_____

_____

_____

_____

_____

5. Thinking of the centurion, why would it be frightening to realise that you have witnessed the death of the Son of God?

_____

_____

_____

_____

6. Are there times when you find it difficult to share what you believe to be true about Jesus? Are there occasions when circumstances make it easier?

_____

_____

_____

_____

Final Thoughts

This story is also told in Matthew 27:45–54. The wording is surprisingly similar but Matthew gives us a few extra details. He mentions the earthquake at the moment of Jesus' death, and the fact that the soldiers were scared (vv51,54).

He also tells us of holy people who had died coming out of their broken tombs and appearing around Jerusalem (vv52–53). What a strange thought – and one that I haven't often heard discussed! Reading Matthew Henry's commentary is enlightening on all the arguments around what may have happened, but helps us to see the reason for mentioning it: the resurrection is for all who have already died as well as those who will; and it is an immediate demonstration of what the crucifixion achieves, even before the resurrection of Jesus Himself has been witnessed.

The purpose of the cross is to bring life. Finding the truth that Jesus is the Son of God helps us make sense of this paradox.

Closing Prayer

Crucified and risen Jesus,
Thank You that You are the way, the truth and the life.
Thank You that You liberate us from darkness.
We want to know You better.
We want to see others as You do.
We want to shout about who You are.
Help us to share Your love and truth.
Amen.

Further Reflection

Matthew tells us of another centurion who discovers the truth and finds faith in Jesus. Read Matthew 8:5–13.

If you want to read more from Matthew Henry's commentary on the whole Bible (1706), you can find it online or in bookshops. The complete version runs to six volumes, but there is also a concise version.

[1] Matthew Henry's commentary can be found at www.biblestudytools.com/commentaries/matthew-henry-complete (accessed July 2016).

The Criminal: Finding Forgiveness

Luke 23:32-43

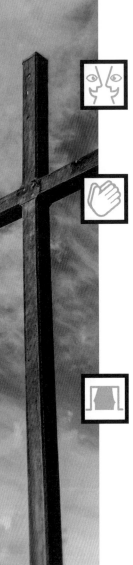

Icebreaker

If you're comfortable doing so, share with the group one thing you have done that was against the law and how you feel about it. If you can't think of anything, choose instead something you've done that you deem to be 'wrong'.

Opening Prayer

All-seeing God, we know that we have fallen short of Your standards.
All-knowing God, we are sorry for the ways we have spoiled Your image in us.
All-loving God, thank You for not giving up on us despite our failure.
All-gracious God, help us discern what is right so we might reflect Your glory each day.
Amen.

Setting the Scene

At the time Jesus lived, Jerusalem was part of the Roman Empire. There were many forms of citizenship, but all had to be applied for and granted. A Roman citizen could only be sentenced to death for treason, and even then, could not be crucified. Anyone suffering this kind of execution was therefore not a citizen of Rome. This made them likely to be of lower education, lower income, different religion, or any other number of factors that meant their rights were limited. (They were unlikely to be slaves, though, as you would choose a punishment that would allow a full recovery for a valuable worker.)

Some historians say that crucifixion, a particularly brutal form of punishment, was used as a political weapon. The Romans were the only ones to do it. It was a sign to anyone posing a threat or challenge to the Empire itself. Many tens of thousands were apparently killed in this way, convicted of insurgency, as a sign to others of what would follow any act of dissension or rebellion.

The justification for the sentence Jesus received was that He had been claiming to be the king of a kingdom superior to Rome. The name given to the others crucified with Him is translated literally as 'malefactors' or 'evil-doers'. It was a name given to some who refused Roman authority. Some have considered they may be associates of Barabbas (who was released in place of Jesus during His trial). Barabbas was a known revolutionary, who had committed murder and incited an insurrection against Roman rule (Luke 23:19).

Those being crucified with Jesus would not have been innocent. In fact, we believe that, apart from Jesus, no one is without sin. But we are left to imagine the details of their crimes. We do hear, however, that Pilate feels Jesus has done no wrong worthy of punishment. Those who want Him dead use the excuse, 'he stirs up the people', knowing it will be the crime that will see Him crucified (Luke 23:4–5).

Bible Readings

Luke 23:32–43

'Two others also, who were criminals, were led away to be put to death with him. When they came to the place that is called The Skull, they crucified Jesus there with the criminals, one on his right and one on his left. Then Jesus said, "Father, forgive them; for they do not know what they are doing." And they cast lots to divide his clothing. And the people stood by, watching; but the leaders scoffed at him, saying, "He saved others; let him save himself if he is the Messiah of God, his chosen one!" The soldiers also mocked him, coming up and offering him sour wine, and saying, "If you are the King of the Jews, save yourself!" There was also an inscription over him, "This is the King of the Jews."

One of the criminals who were hanged there kept deriding him and saying, "Are you not the Messiah? Save yourself and us!" But the other rebuked him,

saying, "Do you not fear God, since you are under the same sentence of condemnation? And we indeed have been condemned justly, for we are getting what we deserve for our deeds, but this man has done nothing wrong." Then he said, "Jesus, remember me when you come into your kingdom." He replied, "Truly I tell you, today you will be with me in Paradise.""

1 John 1:7–9
'but if we walk in the light as he himself is in the light, we have fellowship with one another, and the blood of Jesus his Son cleanses us from all sin. If we say that we have no sin, we deceive ourselves, and the truth is not in us. If we confess our sins, he who is faithful and just will forgive us our sins and cleanse us from all unrighteousness.'

John 3:16
'For God so loved the world that he gave his only son, so that everyone who believes in him may not perish but may have eternal life.'

Session Focus

The criminal on the cross – an imagined address to his mother

You're here. Thanks for coming. I wanted to say I'm sorry. I'm sorry you have to see this. I'm sorry I let you down. I'm sorry I hurt people. Spent too much time and effort making trouble.

I didn't set out to be here. It wasn't a part of some plan. Guess I just got carried away. Got easier as time went on to take bigger risks, fight bigger enemies. Got in with the wrong crowd, as they say.

I promise you, I never roughed anyone up beyond what they asked for, never took from a child, never hit a woman. You taught me right. But I'm not innocent. I made a target

*of those that could afford it, seemed fair that way, sharing
things out. I wanted to make things even. How it should be.
Wasn't my job to do it. Not in the way I did.*

*I don't want to be here. I'm scared. But I knew the score.
I know you wanted better for me and I let you down.
None of this is your fault, I'm a big boy.*

*You see this guy in the middle? He was the real deal.
I believe that sign above his head. Please, Mum, believe
it. There's something royal about him – never imagined
anyone could be such a gentleman in death, 'specially
when people were saying things like they did. Idiot over
there joined in. As if he hadn't landed himself in enough
trouble. So close and so far.*

*I can read a person, had plenty of practice. And that one
in the middle was see-through. Got no 'side'. Clear. Pure.
Gone now already. I asked him to remember me, when
things get put right. You won't believe it, but he told me I'd
be with him in paradise. Today. Paradise! Can you imagine
a place like that? A place where a guy like that is in charge
and no one wants for anything? I want to be there. As
much as I don't deserve it, I believe in it.*

*I'm still so scared. Of the pain and everything else. But
kind of... hopeful. Like maybe God has the big picture even
though I don't. Please don't worry about me.*

*I'm tired now. Tired of fighting. Tired of running. It's
time to stop.*

The word 'atonement' in a theological sense refers to the
reconciliation of God with humankind through Jesus Christ,
particularly in His death and resurrection. There are many
ways to explain and understand exactly how it works and
theologians have debated the nuances during the last two
thousand years.

However we might approach it, it remains central to Jesus'
death and resurrection that His actions achieve forgiveness for
all who will receive it. We can say that, because of this moment,
we are forgiven all our wrongs and made right with God.

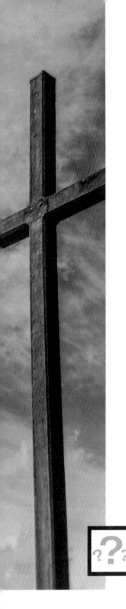

The two criminals show us the potential polar responses to this offer of forgiveness. One shouts, 'Save yourself and us'; he mocks Jesus, neither sorry for his own actions nor believing in Jesus' power to save. The other man's response, however, is quite different.

I find it interesting to note the humility of the criminal in this moment. It's not found in this translation, but in the New King James Version, and in the Greek, he addresses Jesus as 'Lord' or 'Master' (v42). He doesn't ask for forgiveness, he asks to be remembered when Jesus' kingdom is established. In this simple sentence, he demonstrates his understanding that Jesus will hold ultimate authority beyond the justice system of this world.

He has said enough for Jesus to reassure him that today, *today*, there will be a new order and a new world that will welcome him. Jesus calls it 'paradise' (v43). That word evokes a place that sounds so very different from the empire that the insurgents have been desperate to revolt against. It would be a place where all are equal, and citizenship comes via very different criteria. It is already established and open immediately. We imagine it in this instance as an 'afterlife' that begins after our time on earth is over.

In this moment we see the famous words of John 3:16 in practice: 'For God so loved the world that he gave his only son, so that everyone who believes in him may not perish but may have eternal life.'

Discussion Starters

1. What are the things in your society that you would like to change? What are the bases of power that you would like to see overthrown or reformed?

2. Is it our role, as believers, to challenge the laws of our land? If so, how could we go about it?

_____

_____

_____

_____

_____

3. How do you feel about the concept that *all* who truly repent are forgiven? Are there people you think should be *beyond* forgiveness?

_____

_____

_____

_____

4. What is your experience of forgiveness, from God or from others? How has it impacted your subsequent behaviour?

_____

_____

_____

_____

5. Are you usually aware of your wrongdoing? How often do you ask forgiveness from God?

_____

_____

_____

_____

6. What would be 'paradise' for you? How would it differ from this world?

_____

_____

_____

_____

Final Thoughts

Perhaps the key to our forgiveness is humble admittance of our need for it. Thankfully the Holy Spirit can convict us of our wrongdoing when we might be oblivious of it. I think we also have to routinely search our hearts for things we must confess. I like the Anglican liturgies that remind us we sin, 'in thought, word and deed, in what we have done and in what we have left undone'. We sin, 'through negligence, through weakness, through our own deliberate fault'.

We need not dwell upon nor wallow in our failure, but saying sorry and asking to be forgiven reminds us not to take our forgiveness for granted, when Jesus achieved it at such a cost.

It is important to accept forgiveness. Believing that we are not worthy of it is not biblical or helpful; Jesus offers it to all. 1 John 1:9 tells us that, 'If we confess our sins, he who is faithful and just will forgive us our sins and cleanse us from all unrighteousness.'

Closing Prayer

In this prayer, why not leave some time for silence after each line, for individual reflection?

Merciful Father, forgive the wrong we have done knowingly and unknowingly.
Sacrificial Jesus, thank You for the forgiveness You have achieved for us.
Revealing Spirit, convict us of sin and free us from guilt.
Thank You for the chances You give us to try again in this life, and for the promise of paradise to come.
Amen.

STUDY | **TWO**

Further Reflection

The passages often used to help us understand forgiveness through Christ are from Paul's letter to the Romans. Find some time during the week to read the Romans' road to salvation, pausing at each verse to consider your own journey of faith, and pray as you feel appropriate.

Consider: Romans 3:10–12,23; 6:23; 5:8; 10:9–10,13; 5:1; 8:1,38–39.

Joseph of Arimathea: Finding Courage

John 19:38-42

Icebreaker

Take it in turns to answer these two questions:
What are you afraid of?
What gives you courage?

Opening Prayer

Forgive our weakness, Lord. We are so often fearful.
Forgive our negligence, Lord. We are so often quick to give up.
Embolden us, Lord. We long to be brave in Your service.
May we learn from the courage with which You faced the cross.
Amen.

Setting the Scene

This story appears in all four Gospels and although each gives
us slightly different details, they agree on the turn of events.
In addition to John 19, the story also appears at the close of
Matthew 27, Mark 15 and Luke 23. I have chosen to look more
closely at John's account because he includes Nicodemus in
his narrative, along with the principle character, Joseph of
Arimathea. The presence of both men helps shed a little more
light on the challenges of being a member of 'the council'
of leaders of the Jewish people.

Mark tells us that Joseph of Arimathea was a 'respected'
member of this council (Mark 15:43). Matthew tells us he
was 'rich' (Matt. 27:57). Luke chooses to tell us that he was
'good and righteous' (Luke 23:50). Known as the 'Sanhedrin',
the council was a tribunal, or court of justice, comprising a
high priest, chief priests, elders, scribes, and other experts in
the law, such as Pharisees.

Jesus is questioned by this council more than once,
including in the run up to His crucifixion. 'When day came,
the assembly of the elders of the people, both chief priests
and scribes, gathered together, and they brought him to their
council' (Luke 22:66).

These two, Joseph of Arimathea and Nicodemus, are the only two members of this ruling council recorded as having a positive response to Jesus. Nicodemus goes in search of Jesus in the night – resulting in what is probably the most quoted biblical conversation about being born again (John 3:1–21). Otherwise, throughout the Gospels, this council is not sympathetic to Jesus. Threatened and unbelieving, they are primarily responsible for the confusion of His trial and inciting the crowd to lobby Pilate for the resulting crucifixion. This is after Nicodemus seeks to remind his council peers that in accordance with Jewish law, Jesus deserves a fair trial before condemnation, but is dismissed and belittled (John 7:45–52).

Bible Readings

John 19:38–42

'After these things, Joseph of Arimathea, who was a disciple of Jesus, though a secret one because of his fear of the Jews, asked Pilate to let him take away the body of Jesus. Pilate gave him permission; so he came and removed his body. Nicodemus, who had at first come to Jesus by night, also came, bringing a mixture of myrrh and aloes, weighing about a hundred pounds. They took the body of Jesus and wrapped it with the spices in linen cloths, according to the burial custom of the Jews. Now there was a garden in the place where he was crucified, and in the garden there was a new tomb in which no one had ever been laid. And so, because it was the Jewish day of Preparation, and the tomb was nearby, they laid Jesus there.'

John 7:45–52

'Then the temple police went back to the chief priests and Pharisees, who asked them, "Why did you not arrest him?" The police answered, "Never has anyone spoken like this!" Then the Pharisees replied, "Surely you have not been deceived too, have you? Has any one of the authorities or of the Pharisees believed in him?

But this crowd, which does not know the law—they are accursed." Nicodemus, who had gone to Jesus before, and who was one of them, asked, "Our law does not judge people without first giving them a hearing to find out what they are doing, does it?" They replied, "Surely you are not also from Galilee, are you? Search and you will see that no prophet is to arise from Galilee.'"

Session Focus

Joseph of Arimathea – an imagined address to the lifeless body of Jesus, still on the cross

What did I do? More to the point, what did I not do?
I didn't agree but I didn't make my voice heard.
I'm sorry. I'm so very sorry. I'm a coward and now it's too late.
How could I be so scared of them when you were not? At least, you didn't seem scared. You didn't open your mouth to defend yourself and I didn't open my mouth to defend you either. You had most cause to be fearful but thought little of protecting yourself. Unlike me.
I failed to speak up for you. I suspected I might have one ally, but what are two against so many? I knew your kingdom was coming and we'd all be found wanting, but I didn't know it would end this way, especially not this soon. I thought I had more time. I thought I'd have a chance to convince them, or that you would. Now it's too late.
I wish I could do right by you. I may have failed you so far but I can do something now. There isn't much time. I'll go to Pilate, I can do that more readily than your friends. I'll ask if I can bury you, you deserve that much at least. I'll save your body if not your life, and bring you the dignity you've been denied.
I'll need spices and cloths. I'll need to move quickly.
I'll need help. Will you allow me to do this for you? I know somewhere. It's not far from here. It's a peaceful spot

in a garden. A far cry from this desolation and yet only
moments away.
    It's far too little. It's far too late. Will you allow me?
It's the least I can do.

John tells us that Joseph was a 'secret' disciple of Jesus, 'for fear of the Jews' (v38). The other versions of the story echo this sentiment of fear. Mark uses the word 'boldly' to describe Joseph's approach to Pilate (v43), but clearly he is not so bold with his colleagues. Luke tells us that Joseph had not consented to the actions of the council (v1). There were over seventy members of the Sanhedrin, so being the dissenting voice would have been a considerable challenge.

We often hear that Jesus died for those whose voices are not heard, and we think of those who lack a 'platform' or opportunity to speak. One of the things I appreciate most about this story is the reminder that however influential someone may seem to be, they may still struggle, perhaps all the more, to stand up for what they believe to be right. The places where the opportunity is biggest can also be the places where it costs the most to speak out against the majority. It's in these situations that we must entrust ourselves to Jesus, who let His actions speak louder than words. In this case, Joseph of Arimathea manages with his actions to do what he was unable to do by speech – contributing to the building of the kingdom of God by giving honour to Jesus, and fulfilling the scriptural prophecy of God's big plan in the process.

Joseph takes Jesus' body to a nearby garden for burial. He is pressed for time before the sun sets – funerals were not permitted on the Sabbath. Someone crucified for sedition would not be released to the next of kin for burial, they would be left to rot or thrown in a criminals' communal grave. In Isaiah 53, where the death of Jesus is described many years before His life, we are tolds that, 'They made his grave with the wicked and his tomb with the rich' (v9). Although His death should have put Him in amongst a heap of criminals, He ends up in the tomb of a rich man, buried as one worthy of royal treatment.

In addition, just as death enters the world in a garden in Genesis, so death will be conquered by resurrection in a garden. 'For just as by the one man's disobedience the many were made sinners, so by the one man's obedience the many will be made righteous' (Rom. 5:19).

Discussion Starters

1. Has there been a time when you have needed courage to stand up for something you believe to be important or right?

_____
_____
_____

2. How hard or easy do you find it to voice an opinion that differs from the majority around you?

_____
_____
_____
_____
_____

3. Where are the places of opportunity for you to speak up for Jesus?

_____
_____
_____
_____
_____

4. What are the things that you would have to sacrifice, or risk, to speak out?

_____
_____
_____
_____
_____

5. How might you overcome some of the obstacles to speaking
up or being heard?

_____

_____

_____

_____

_____

6. If you cannot speak, what are the reasons? And how might
you be able to act instead?

_____

_____

_____

_____

_____

Final Thoughts

If you are working through these studies as part of a group,
spend some time praying for those who feel they need courage.
Find out what they want to stand for and why it is tough.
Commit to praying for them during this week and remember
to ask next week if they have anything to share in response.

Have you thought before about the echoes of Jesus' death
and resurrection seen in the Old Testament, written many
years before His life? Isaiah 53 and Psalm 22 are probably
the best known passages where this occurs. You might like
to close your eyes and listen to someone reading them aloud
while you allow your mind to explore the echoes. How might
they affect your thinking about the crucifixion? Jesus was
certainly very familiar with the Old Testament, and the
Pharisees are likely to have known the Scriptures very well
(the disciples perhaps less so, although growing in knowledge).
I believe their responses to the events of the Passion are
affected, and so might ours be.

Closing Prayer

Jesus, thank You for the triumph over death that You won
through Your resurrection in the garden.
Thank You that You are always with us.
Help us find strength and courage to stand up for others.
Help us find strength and courage to stand up for You.
Give us the wisdom, the words and the wherewithal to do
what is right in Your eyes.
Amen.

Further Reflection

If you want to read the synoptic accounts of this story you can
find them here:

> Matthew 27:57–61
> Mark 15:42–47
> Luke 23:50–56

In addition, you could look at the story of Nicodemus'
night-time encounter with Jesus in John 3 and consider the
difficulty of standing up against a powerful majority.

You may want to download or buy an audio Bible to hear
the passages read aloud to you. The NIV Audio Bible is
excellently voiced by David Suchet.

Mary: Finding Trust

Luke 2:25–38

Icebreaker

Are you good at waiting, or not so good? Do you remember the Guinness slogan, 'Good things come to those who wait'? Share what has been the best or worst thing to wait for in your life so far.

Opening Prayer

God of today and all ages,
God of the known and unknown,
God of the seen and unseen,
teach us to trust You.
Be in our waiting.
Guide us in prayer.
Expand our patience.
Help us to live one day at a time, looking to You.
Amen.

Setting the Scene

Mary plays her starring role at the birth of Jesus. We hear she is 'favoured' by God and entrusted with growing, delivering and raising the person who will be God's hope for the salvation of humanity (Luke 1:30). She then goes on to have a quiet but constant presence through the rest of Jesus' life and beyond into the Early Church.

She is someone who knows the Scriptures – her song of praise in Luke 1 is improvised around Hannah's prayer from 1 Samuel 2 with other passages mixed in. Her thirst for God's Word can only have increased with the knowledge that her child was to be His hope for the redemption of Israel.

We often hear that the death of a child is one of the most difficult things anyone can face, but Mary has known so much of God's intervention in her life, and seen Him at work in her unusual son, so surely she cannot fail to trust Him now too.

Her example of trust to me is reflected in other godly characters throughout the Bible, including Simeon and Anna who we're going to read about in today's study. It comes down to waiting and praying. The waiting and praying is motivated by the belief that God is good and will keep His promises. Of course this is helped by a knowledge of His promises – something which spurs me on to read more of the Old Testament alongside the New.

The crucifixion and resurrection are the moments when all Scripture is fulfilled and God's big picture begins to make sense as the puzzle pieces are all put in place. Those who have been waiting and praying will see the moment, whether they realise it at the time or not.

Bible Readings

Luke 2:25–38

'Now there was a man in Jerusalem whose name was Simeon; this man was righteous and devout, looking forward to the consolation of Israel, and the Holy Spirit rested on him. It had been revealed to him by the Holy Spirit that he would not see death before he had seen the Lord's Messiah. Guided by the Spirit, Simeon came into the temple; and when the parents brought in the child Jesus, to do for him what was customary under the law, Simeon took him in his arms and praised God, saying,

"Master, now you are dismissing your servant in peace, according to your word; for my eyes have seen your salvation, which you have prepared in the presence of all peoples, a light for revelation to the Gentiles and for glory to your people Israel."

And the child's father and mother were amazed at what was being said about him. Then Simeon blessed them and said to his mother Mary, "This child is destined for the falling and the rising of many in Israel, and to be a sign that will be opposed so that the inner thoughts of many will be revealed—and a sword will pierce your own soul too."

There was also a prophet, Anna the daughter of Phanuel, of the tribe of Asher. She was of a great age, having lived with her husband seven years after her marriage, then as a widow to the age of eighty-four. She never left the temple but worshiped there with fasting and prayer night and day. At that moment she came, and began to praise God and to speak about the child to all who were looking for the redemption of Jerusalem.'

Luke 1:46–55
'And Mary said,
  "My soul magnifies the Lord,
    and my spirit rejoices in God my Savior,
  for he has looked with favor on the lowliness
  of his servant.
    Surely, from now on all generations will
    call me blessed;
  for the Mighty One has done great things for me,
    and holy is his name.
  His mercy is for those who fear him
    from generation to generation.
  He has shown strength with his arm;
    he has scattered the proud in the thoughts
    of their hearts.
  He has brought down the powerful from their thrones,
    and lifted up the lowly;
  he has filled the hungry with good things,
    and sent the rich away empty.
  He has helped his servant Israel,
    in remembrance of his mercy,
  according to the promise he made to our ancestors,
    to Abraham and to his descendants forever."'

Session Focus

Mary – an imagined address to John, by her side at the cross

I've never doubted him. How could I? The way he was conceived. The things that happened in his early years. The man he became.

I stored up all the things that happened, everything that was said. I kept them in my heart and mind and they're all tumbling over each other now. 'A sword will pierce your own soul too.' I feel it. Oh, I feel it.

I couldn't imagine that his time would come before mine. I have faithfully followed my son, never dreaming it would be my honour to see his whole life.

Oh, the pain of this!

I feel as though each tear in his skin, each drop of his blood is mine.

We went through so much to protect him. Blocking out the whispers and rumours. Finding our own way. Two years of asylum in Egypt, running through the night.

The foreign visitors brought myrrh. For healing. For anointing. For embalming. For a High Priest and King who didn't look like one then and doesn't look like one now. But he is, I know it.

You'll think I'm crazy, but I'll say it again, 'The Mighty One has done great things for me. His name is holy.'

This has to be part of the story that we must endure. It has to be a stepping stone to the kingdom we've been waiting for. It has to be for the redemption of Israel. God is always working towards his purposes. He is and I know it, John. I don't want it to be true! Please, God, let there be another way! But I have to believe it.

I cannot hold on to my child. He is not mine. He never was. It has been my great joy to nurture him and he has given me more than I could ever offer in return. I have to put him in the hands of the Lord where he belongs. I can do no other even though it breaks my heart. I can't look at this.

We must pray and remember him as he was. And wait for the Lord. It is all that is left to do.

A young couple turn up to the Temple for a 'routine' thanksgiving for their firstborn and find two wise and elderly prophets (unrelated to each other) who have been waiting and praying for the promised Messiah. They both go slightly crackers in this moment – God has told them this is the one! Not only the one to bring salvation to the Jews, but also to be a light to the gentiles. This is going to be a far wider redemption than first expected and it's in the shape of a baby – currently utterly dependent on parental care. Moments like these must have had a lasting impact on Mary, who is piecing together a picture of God's redemption plan – with parts of the puzzle still unknown. There is more waiting to come to understand the words spoken.

As the story of Jesus' life unfolds, there are epic highs and devastating lows – all part of the fullness of life that Mary seems to embrace. The most peace-filled people I know are able to accept all that comes their way with the knowledge that God is with them. 'Shall we receive the good at the hand of God, and not receive the bad?' (Job 2:10).

Job, and many others, continue a discourse with God throughout their suffering. Mary is no doubt one of these. She is certainly prayerful. In the life of the Early Church she is described as one of those 'constantly devot[ed]' to prayer. 'All these were constantly devoting themselves to prayer, together with certain women, including Mary the mother of Jesus, as well as his brothers' (Acts 1:14).

Matthew Henry's commentary on Simeon in our first passage reminds us how important it is that he is now willing to be 'dismissed in peace'. He says, 'Those that have welcomed Christ may welcome death'.[1] We will think about this more in the last session, but I think Mary's trust has a similar impact; knowing Jesus and His saving power makes death infinitely less threatening. Waiting and praying has so far revealed that God's will is done in the end, whatever happens in the meantime.

Discussion Starters

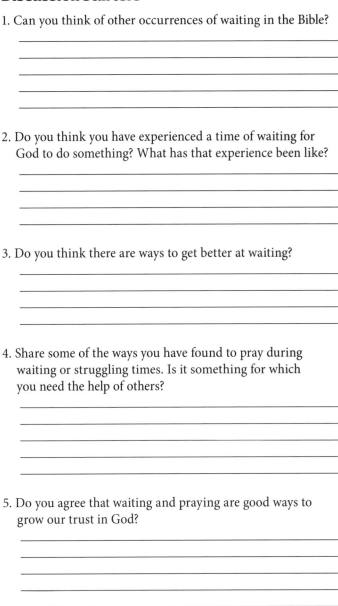

1. Can you think of other occurrences of waiting in the Bible?

_____
_____
_____
_____
_____

2. Do you think you have experienced a time of waiting for
   God to do something? What has that experience been like?

_____
_____
_____
_____

3. Do you think there are ways to get better at waiting?

_____
_____
_____
_____

4. Share some of the ways you have found to pray during
   waiting or struggling times. Is it something for which
   you need the help of others?

_____
_____
_____
_____
_____

5. Do you agree that waiting and praying are good ways to
   grow our trust in God?

_____
_____
_____
_____

6. How else might our trust in God be increased?

_____

_____

_____

_____

Final Thoughts

You may have heard Tony Campolo's phrase, 'It's Friday but Sunday's coming.' The days between Good Friday and Easter Sunday, when Jesus is dead but not yet raised, feel dark and difficult. In human suffering, we understand what it is to wait for God's intervention, and He understands our pain.

You have probably also heard of the theology that we live in 'the now and not yet'. Ours is a time when Jesus has conquered, but has not yet returned to judge the living and the dead and put all things right. We are in a waiting time.

That's not to say we are inactive. The Psalms are full of exhortations to 'wait for the Lord', and Psalm 130:6 tells us how active this waiting is: 'My soul waits for the Lord, more than those who watch for the morning, more than those who watch for the morning.' We are to be eagerly seeking for God's will to be done, joining with His mission to build His kingdom on earth. We do all of this in a time of struggle, sorrow and heartache until the day when Jesus returns to 'wipe every tear' from our eyes (Rev. 21:4).

It is by prayerfully getting on with whatever we face every day that we learn to trust God to fulfil His purposes.

Closing Prayer

Good and holy God: Father, Son and Spirit,
We put ourselves in Your hands.
Thank You for keeping Your promises.
Thank You for hearing our spoken and unspoken prayers.
Please meet us in our waiting.
We praise You for the death and resurrection of Jesus that was all according to Your plan.
Thank You that it changes everything for us and all of humankind.
Amen.

Further Reflection

I believe the following once took place during an interview with Mother Teresa.

'When you pray, what do you say to God?'

'I don't talk, I simply listen.'

'And what does God say to you?'

'He also doesn't talk, He simply listens.'[2]

Try waiting for God in silent prayer. Start with a minute and increase by a minute each time, perhaps daily or weekly.

---

[1] Matthew Henry's commentary, found at www.biblestudytools.com/commentaries/matthew-henry-complete/luke/2.html (accessed July 2016).

[2] Found at www.soundfaith.com/sermons/79049-mother-teresa-on-listening (accessed July 2016).

Thaddaeus:
Finding Faith under Fire
Matthew 10:1-8, 16-25

Icebreaker

Tell the group about the most unusual or surprising reaction you had from someone when they discovered that you were a Christian, or when they discovered something else about you that they didn't previously know. It might have been funny or upsetting.

Opening Prayer

Almighty God, You are our strength and our defender.
When things seem hopeless and we feel helpless, You are there.
Remind us of Your presence when we feel alone or weak.
Strengthen our faith in You, that we might face all we must.
Bless and protect all those facing persecution for their belief in You today.
Amen.

Setting the Scene

The twelve disciples were not the only disciples of Jesus. Many followed Him; many travelled with Him, listened to Him and learned from Him. All sorts of people are described as disciples. However, Jesus chose these twelve to be His 'A-Team' of constant companions. They learned by 'doing life' alongside Jesus. We hear more of some than others, but this passage shows how all twelve were far more than spectators – their training with this rather unconventional master was a white-knuckle ride unlike any other. Jesus never promises them it will be easy, but instead prepares them for hardship.

We don't know how many of the Twelve witnessed the crucifixion. We are only told of the presence of women and of John (John 19:26). Others may have been in hiding for fear of their own safety; Peter perhaps nursing the shame of his denial. I like to imagine some were there but trying to keep a low profile, not standing together and trying to blend in. The chaos of the hours since they ate the Passover meal together, the lack of sleep, the quick and overwhelming turn of events and confusion in their minds may have scattered them. There was no plan for this. We know they gather after the event, huddling together in a locked room in Jerusalem (John 20:19), but for this part of the story, they are isolated.

In seeking a voice from amongst those closest to Jesus, I've chosen to think about Thaddaeus. I find it useful to consider someone we know less about because it reminds me to think of the big picture, rather than the specific incidents we are often more familiar with.

Bible Reading

Matthew 10:1–8,16–25

'Then Jesus summoned his twelve disciples and gave them authority over unclean spirits, to cast them out, and to cure every disease and every sickness. These are the names of the twelve apostles: first, Simon, also known as Peter, and his brother Andrew; James son of Zebedee, and his brother John; Philip and Bartholomew; Thomas and Matthew the tax collector; James son of Alphaeus, and Thaddaeus; Simon the Cananaean, and Judas Iscariot, the one who betrayed him.

These twelve Jesus sent out with the following instructions: "Go nowhere among the Gentiles, and enter no town of the Samaritans, but go rather to the lost sheep of the house of Israel. As you go, proclaim the good news, 'The kingdom of heaven has come near.' Cure the sick, raise the dead, cleanse the lepers, cast out demons. You received without payment; give without payment … See, I am sending you out like sheep into the midst of wolves; so be wise as serpents and innocent as doves. Beware of them, for they will hand you over to councils and flog you in their synagogues; and you will be dragged before governors and kings because of me, as a testimony to them and the Gentiles. When they hand you over, do not worry about how you are to speak or what you are to say; for what you are to say will be given to you at that time; for it is not you who speak, but the Spirit of

your Father speaking through you. Brother will betray brother to death, and a father his child, and children will rise against parents and have them put to death; and you will be hated by all because of my name. But the one who endures to the end will be saved. When they persecute you in one town, flee to the next; for truly I tell you, you will not have gone through all the towns of Israel before the Son of Man comes. A disciple is not above the teacher, nor a slave above the master; it is enough for the disciple to be like the teacher, and the slave like the master. If they have called the master of the house Beelzebul, how much more will they malign those of his household!'"

Session Focus

Thaddaeus – an imagined address to Jesus on the cross

Master, I can't bear to see you like this. Do something! Is this what you meant by loving your enemies? You could stop this at any moment. Your kingdom is meant to be coming.

This has been the longest day of my life, waiting for a miracle that will surely come. But when? You're the only thing I've ever been certain of and now what? Who am I without you?

Three years. Three years since you strolled up to me on the beach and said, 'Are you coming or what?' The best three years. I want to forget for a minute that they led here. Just a few weeks ago, on a normal afternoon, a boy came back to life at my request. Four women were healed, an old man and six children. A whole family was freed from a possessive spirit because you were right behind me. But now ... I've never felt so helpless. We're not even all together. How can we continue alone?

You said we'd be persecuted because of you. Well, who's going to care about the one-time followers of a dead man? I would've died for you! We all would. It would make much more sense to sacrifice one of us to the cause. There is no

*cause without you. When I've thought about persecution
and tried to imagine what might happen, I never thought
about anything like this. I can't even look. Is it us next?
I thought I could take it so long as you were there too.*

*You can keep calling me 'Thaddeus the quiet one'
because I don't know what to say. I don't understand how
this works as part of the plan. How do I become like you,
now? Do I give myself up for death? What will it gain? Do
I try to keep doing what you started? I want to endure to
the end like you told us, but is it the end already? I can't
imagine how far we might take your teaching from here,
how long we might last. Not far enough. You'd better have
something planned to sustain us. I know you probably do.
Your words are echoing and bouncing round my head but I
can't make sense of it all.*

Don't leave us, Master. Jesus. Please.

Being the disciple of a rabbi, particularly one of the inner circle,
involved close proximity to the rabbi in question. The aim was
to learn to be like them, not just imitating their public life, but
knowing how they approached all of life's tasks. There would
be a knowledge that at some point it would be time to function
without the constant presence of the rabbi, but I wonder if the
crucifixion felt too soon a separation for the Twelve. There is
always so much to learn.

One thing that is clear is that Jesus is preparing them for
coming trials. He never promises that following Him will be
the easy option; 'the gate is narrow and the road is hard that
leads to life, and there are few who find it' (Matt. 7:14).

Jesus tells them, 'They will hand you over to be tortured
and will put you to death, and you will be hated by all nations
because of my name' (Matt. 24:9). We are to expect hardship as
followers of Jesus. The crucifixion was the proof that Jesus was
prepared to face first what we might all face for our faith. He
does not ask of us what He has not been willing to do Himself.
Many of the disciples went on to be martyred, and indeed there
are many facing death for their faith today.

John 16 tells us that Jesus had more to say but didn't feel like the disciples could take it all in (v12), and He hopes that they will remember His words 'when the hour comes' (v4). The important thing for them to remember is that they are not alone, even in the physical absence of the Saviour. Jesus tells them that the Father is present (v32), and that the Holy Spirit will come (v7). Therefore it is actually to their advantage that He should leave them, however unwilling they are to face it.

Discussion Starters

1. How do you think that God understands human suffering? Why might He expect us to face it?

_____

_____

_____

_____

_____

2. Do you feel or sense the presence of God with you in times of trouble? If so, how?

_____

_____

_____

_____

_____

3. Do you think Christians are persecuted in your community? In what ways?

_____

_____

_____

_____

_____

4. In what ways do you think facing death is frightening? Is it something you ever consider?

_____
_____
_____
_____
_____

5. How might we remember the words of Jesus at times when it matters most?

_____
_____
_____
_____
_____

6. Do you ever feel alone in your Christian life? How can we avoid that loneliness?

_____
_____
_____
_____
_____

Final Thoughts

We don't know whether the disciples understood what was going to happen next, though I suspect they knew the story wasn't over.

We are told that the chief priests knew what had been foretold: 'we remember what that impostor said while he was still alive, "After three days I will rise again." Therefore command the tomb to be made secure until the third day; otherwise his disciples may go and steal him away, and tell the people, "He has been raised from the dead," and the last deception would be worse than the first' (Matt. 27:62–64).

We know that the disciples gather together in fear to pray and wait, and as the story unfolds on the Sunday morning

there is great excitement. It is the resurrection and the presence of God's power with each one of them, particularly after the day of Pentecost when the Spirit fills them (Acts 2), which makes them able to do what they go on to do and face the struggles ahead.

The cross is the first demonstration and reminder of this constant encouragement from Jesus: 'In the world you face persecution. But take courage; I have conquered the world!' (John 16:33).

Closing Prayer

Holy Spirit, thank You that You are always with us.
Give us strength and grace as we face trials of all kinds.
May we cling to faith in Jesus, and not to false comfort.
Help us to find the right attitude towards our own lives.
Protect us from evil and show us how to stand for God's purposes around the world.
Amen.

Further Reflection

Have a look at the website of Open Doors UK (www.opendoorsuk.org) and see the 'World Watch List' of countries where it is most costly to follow Christ. Commit to spending some time in prayer for our church family around the world who live in daily fear for their lives.

Martha: Finding Life

John 11:17-27

Icebreaker

Share with the group what age you have most enjoyed being. If you could be one age forever, would it be that one? Why?

Opening Prayer

Creator God, we thank You for the years of life You give us. May we seek to worship and serve You in all our years to come.

Living God, we thank You for the years that Jesus lived as a man. May we understand more of His life and death.

Saviour God, we thank You for the promise of eternity with You. As we consider the death of Your Son, help us find life in Him. Amen.

Setting the Scene

In his Gospel, John is concerned with 'signs'. He gathers evidence in support of Jesus' identity as Saviour and tells the stories of those who discover it. In the first ten chapters we see miracles and testimonies, resulting in wide discussions about who this man could be. We hear them trying to figure it out: 'When the Messiah comes, will he do more signs than this man has done?' (John 7:31).

In John 11, the theme continues but it becomes more personal. 'Jesus loved Martha and her sister and Lazarus' (John 11:5). I have always been drawn to this story of Jesus interacting with His close friends; it somehow reminds me of how real and human He was. I can imagine them laughing over a celebratory dinner together, and the atmosphere changing when Mary anointed His feet with perfume and dried them with her hair (John 12:1–3).

Here we will focus on Martha. Best known and often berated for her busyness recorded in Luke 10, here in John 11 she is one of the first to plainly proclaim the truth she has learned of Jesus' identity: 'I believe that you are the Messiah' (John 11:27).

We do not know if she later witnessed the crucifixion. John records that several Marys were there (John 19:25);

Jesus addresses 'daughters of Jerusalem' (Luke 23:27–28) and Luke tells of women from Galilee (Luke 23:49); Matthew confirms women were present (Matt. 27:55), and Mark writes of 'many other women who had come up with him to Jerusalem' (Mark 15:41). We cannot be sure whether Martha was among them. We know she was Jesus' friend and she lived in Bethany, only two miles away from Jerusalem (John 11:18). In the light of this passage, I like to imagine she could not have stayed away. Her memories of what He had said and done, and who she had understood Him to be, would have been tumbling in her mind.

Bible Readings

John 11:17–27

'When Jesus arrived, he found that Lazarus had already been in the tomb four days. Now Bethany was near Jerusalem, some two miles away, and many of the Jews had come to Martha and Mary to console them about their brother. When Martha heard that Jesus was coming, she went and met him, while Mary stayed at home. Martha said to Jesus, "Lord, if you had been here, my brother would not have died. But even now I know that God will give you whatever you ask of him." Jesus said to her, "Your brother will rise again." Martha said to him, "I know that he will rise again in the resurrection on the last day." Jesus said to her, "I am the resurrection and the life. Those who believe in me, even though they die, will live, and everyone who lives and believes in me will never die. Do you believe this?" She said to him, "Yes, Lord, I believe that you are the Messiah, the Son of God, the one coming into the world."'

1 Thessalonians 4:13–18

'But we do not want you to be uninformed, brothers and sisters, about those who have died, so that you may not grieve as others do who have no hope. For since we believe that Jesus died and rose again, even so, through Jesus,

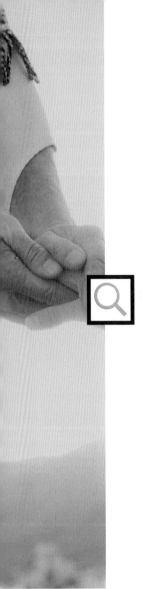

God will bring with him those who have died. For this we declare to you by the word of the Lord, that we who are alive, who are left until the coming of the Lord, will by no means precede those who have died. For the Lord himself, with a cry of command, with the archangel's call and with the sound of God's trumpet, will descend from heaven, and the dead in Christ will rise first. Then we who are alive, who are left, will be caught up in the clouds together with them to meet the Lord in the air; and so we will be with the Lord forever. Therefore encourage one another with these words.'

Session Focus

Martha – an imagined inner monologue at the cross

It would be all very well if it were someone else up there. Jesus would sort them out. Even if they were already dead, he'd have them up and out in time for dinner no matter how long the worms had been at them. But who can do the same for him? He ordered my brother out of the tomb but he won't order his own executioners to stop. He'll command the wind and the waves, but not his killers.

I assume he has a plan. Nothing every phased him and if he still had it in him to talk he might explain. Although he's always had a love of mystery. I can't bear seeing his pain. I know where he's going eventually – where he taught us we're all going. But being confident of the resurrection life in glory is one thing and leaving us here without it is quite another! I'm so angry. He told me off for getting at Mary about helping out with the serving. He said she'd chosen 'that which would not be taken away from her'. Well, he is being taken away! I was right to keep working because life just carries on. Even though it doesn't seem right that it should.

I can still see him walking towards me when I ran to meet him at Lazarus' wake. Death never phased him. It can't worry the Messiah, can it? He wept for his friend, but then he raised him.

Simple.

Easy.

Is this his easy option? Heading for the final trumpet as a man without sin? Waiting to greet us in glory when the time comes? But would he leave us behind to fight the rest of this battle ourselves?

There must be something I'm missing. So much I don't understand.

How can I reconcile who he is with how he looks now – hanging like meat from a hook? Who is he, with life dripping from his body? Should the Messiah look like this? How will he accomplish all the work he promised? What will become of his followers? How will we remember his teaching?

And how will I cope without his friendship?

When Lazarus falls ill, Martha sends word to Jesus – she knows that taking her concerns to Him is the first thing to do. She says, 'Lord, he whom *you love* is ill' (John 11:3, own emphasis). It is echoed in the epistles with, 'Cast all your anxiety on him because he cares for you' (1 Pet. 5:7). As we pray for the sick and care for our friends and family, we remember that God loves them more than we can. What's more, death is unable to separate anyone from that love (Rom. 8:38–39).

In today's reading from John 11, we see that Martha goes to meet Jesus as He arrives, knowing His presence will be a comfort and He will see God's will done, whatever that may be (v22). When Martha tells Mary that Jesus has arrived (v28), it is sometimes translated 'master' and sometimes 'teacher'. The word *didaskalos* is for 'a teaching master'. From his teaching comes comfort and understanding. Martha trusts that Jesus will be able to teach them something new from this experience.

In this community no one is alone in their grief; many come to support Martha and Mary (v19). When Jesus arrives, He too weeps (v35). He is fully human and knows what it is to feel the pain of grief. God is with us in our suffering and we must be with others in theirs. Those present get to see a miracle beyond anything they expected – by being close to the friends of Jesus they also get to be closer to Jesus Himself and see His power at work. Verse 45 tells us that many believed in Him from this moment.

The things that most fill us with despair are often the things God can use to bring glory to Himself. When hope seems lost and circumstances seem unbearable, they are never beyond restoration and redemption for Jesus. His own resurrection happens far beyond the point that anyone expected – He was already in the tomb. His disciples seem to be expecting Him to turn things around all the way through the passion narrative. Then when it seems too late and the stone blocks the tomb – God's big plan is fulfilled and everything is made new.

Discussion Starters

1. When Jesus tells Martha, 'Everyone who lives and believes in me will never die', He follows it up with the direct question, 'Do you believe this?' (John 11:25–26). If He were to ask you, would you find it easy or difficult to respond? What might you say?

   _____

   _____

   _____

   _____

   _____

2. Consider if your answer to this question would be different before and after having knowledge of the resurrection of Jesus.

   _____

   _____

   _____

   _____

3. Martha answers, 'Yes' followed by a declaration that she believes Jesus to be, 'the Messiah, the Son of God' (John 11:27). How can the identity of Jesus bring comfort when we experience the loss of a loved one?

_____

_____

_____

_____

_____

4. Martha had a traditional human friendship with Jesus. Now that He is not physically present in the same way, how might we cultivate a friendship with Him?

_____

_____

_____

_____

_____

5. What benefits do we have in knowing Jesus post-resurrection?

_____

_____

_____

_____

_____

6. How does the concept of eternal life affect how you live today? What do you think resurrection looks like in this world, and in the world to come?

_____

_____

_____

_____

_____

Final Thoughts

1 Thessalonians 4:13–18 sums it up. We do not grieve as those who have no hope. The death and resurrection of Jesus fill us with hope for life in all its fullness, now and beyond this life. Martha knew it was coming, but the death and resurrection of Jesus would drag it closer than she imagined and make it more real and tangible. We see resurrection at work in our lives today at moments when the kingdom of heaven breaks in and God's will is done. People and relationships are restored, and many experience 'new life' where previously things have seemed hopeless. It is important that we understand resurrection is happening all around us. Knowing Jesus brings life in all its fullness to those who were spiritually dead.

For now there is still grief. In fact, it hurts because we are made for eternity. That is why loss is so painful. We cannot understand how the new heaven and earth will look, feel or function, but we live in trust that Jesus will be the King of His kingdom and, as Julian of Norwich famously said, 'All shall be well, and all shall be well, and all manner of thing shall be well'.

Closing Prayer

Lord, thank You for the death of Your Son that brings us life. Give us confidence in the new heaven and earth beyond our time here.
Thank You for the friends and family we love; help us to mourn those we've lost with hope in You.
Thank You for the opportunity of friendship with Jesus. Help us to know that His resurrection is for today.
May we see it in our homes and communities.
Amen.

Further Reflection

Take some time to read the account of the resurrection in John 20.

Consider verse 31: 'But these are written so that you may come to believe that Jesus is the Messiah, the Son of God, and that through believing you may have life in his name.'

Ponder what 'life in his name' is going to mean for you in the coming season.

Leader's Notes

General Notes on Leading the Studies

- Consider your answer for the icebreaker in advance. If you can go first it will save putting others on the spot. If your answer is honest, but not too elaborate, it will reassure others about the kind of response that's helpful and they shouldn't feel intimidated.

- It would be helpful to have Bibles nearby for following the passages or discussing differences in translations. If you have a computer or tablet handy, it can make searching for a particular passage or key word easier. For example, during your discussions, you might want to search for all the references to a particular word or person. You can do this on www.biblegateway.com amongst others, or with various apps.

- Have someone in the group prepare the monologue in advance. It needn't be dramatic, but it will help if they can read it aloud fluently and confidently. Ideally it would be someone different each time. They will gain insight through the preparation, as well as in the discussions. Leave a short pause after the monologue. It is helpful to allow thoughts to wander around the material for a moment before emotions settle and the more cerebral response can continue.

- Spend some time considering the discussion starters in advance so that you may have something to say to kick-start the conversation if others are nervous or need some help.

- Time-keeping will be important in a group discussion. Keep an eye on progress and try to stop at the promised end time. Decide which sections you feel are most important to explore together and which sections can be an individual follow-up later on. You don't need to stick to the studies exactly as they are; allow the discussion to wander, led by

the Holy Spirit and the needs of the group. If it feels like you've wandered away from a useful reflection for Lent, do pull it back to topic.

• Don't feel that you can only pray with the words suggested in each prayer section. It would be good to leave time for your own prayers for yourselves and each other.

STUDY ONE:
The Centurion: Finding Truth

• The focus for this session is discovering the truth of who Jesus is, and being able to make a public declaration about our belief.

• Spiritual darkness and light are also a theme running through that may be interesting to explore further.

• There may be time for someone to share a testimony of how they came to believe in Jesus.

• If you want to do some reading and research in preparation, Matthew Henry's commentary on the selected passage is very useful. I found it online at www.biblestudytools.com/commentaries/matthew-henry-complete

STUDY TWO:
The Criminal: Finding Forgiveness

• The key topic for this session is forgiveness – it may be a rather obvious topic regarding the crucifixion, but vital nonetheless. It is often a subject that creates vibrant debate when we consider our own attitudes to who may or may not 'deserve' forgiveness.

• It is crucial to our individual and corporate faith to ask for forgiveness, and to receive it. Having an opportunity to do this in a trusted group or prayer triplet can be beneficial.

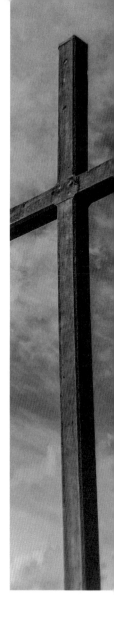

- A secondary theme here is the nature of heaven – when it might begin and what it might be like. A place where forgiveness is no longer necessary may perhaps be a hard concept for us to grasp, but fun to imagine.

STUDY THREE:
Joseph of Arimathea: Finding Courage

- The detail of this session is structured around having courage to do the right thing, particularly standing up for our faith. For many in the workplace, or at home, it can be daunting to go against the flow. Try to create an encouraging environment where small victories are celebrated.

- It may be an opportunity to make a decision or resolution about a time, place or situation where we want to have more courage, particularly in sharing our faith.

STUDY FOUR:
Mary: Finding Trust

- The subject for this session is trust in God. My suggestion is that a knowledge that He is good, and a willingness to wait and pray for the fulfilment of His purposes, however bleak things may seem, is what trust looks like in practical terms. There may be other opinions about what it means to trust God and all are equally valid.

- Our experiences can affect our trust in God – try to encourage some personal testimony of times where this has happened in a positive way. There may also be some who have struggled to trust God, and these stories are also important to hear.

- It may be unusual to explore a little of the Christmas narrative at Easter. Remember that Jesus didn't go straight from Christmas to Easter in one annual cycle as we do – there were many years in between. But it can be useful to

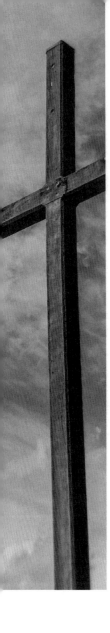

draw parallels between the events and think about how the story fits together.

STUDY FIVE:
Thaddaeus: Finding Faith under Fire

- In this session we will think about persecution, particularly the challenges we may face in life due to our relationship with Jesus and the things He calls us to do. Christianity is certainly a hope and joy-filled journey, but Jesus also prepares us for pain and struggle. Try to keep a balance in the discussion.

- The presence of God with us, by His Holy Spirit, is the secondary theme here. We do not face trials alone. Perhaps someone could share a testimony about knowing His presence in a time of struggle, particularly if that knowledge came with hindsight. Jesus felt abandoned on the cross and cried out to God, asking why He had been forsaken (Mark 15:34). And yet He knew that this was part of the plan and had prayed, 'yet, not my will but yours be done' the night before His death (Luke 22:42). *Knowing* God is with us and *feeling* like it can be two different things.

- It may be worth doing some research on the persecuted church via www.opendoorsuk.org before taking a look at it with your group.

STUDY SIX:
Martha: Finding Life

- The cross, although an instrument of pain and suffering, is to us a symbol of hope. In this session, we consider the paradox that in Jesus life comes through death.

- Some pastoral sensitivity may be needed, particularly if anyone is recently bereaved. Many will have experienced the loss of a friend or relative and have strong feelings about grief. Endeavour to involve everyone in the conversation, and again, keep a balance in the discussion.

• What resurrection life looks like (both in this life and 'the next') may be a tricky concept to imagine, but hopefully pressing on with the discussion will yield interesting thoughts and ideas.

Notes

The bestselling *Cover to Cover* Bible Study Series

1 Corinthians
Growing a Spirit-filled church
ISBN: 978-1-85345-374-8

2 Corinthians
Restoring harmony
ISBN: 978-1-85345-551-3

1 Peter
Good reasons for hope
ISBN: 978-1-78259-088-0

2 Peter
Living in the light of God's promises
ISBN: 978-1-78259-403-1

1 Timothy
Healthy churches –
effective Christians
ISBN: 978-1-85345-291-8

23rd Psalm
The Lord is my shepherd
ISBN: 978-1-85345-449-3

2 Timothy and Titus
Vital Christianity
ISBN: 978-1-85345-338-0

Abraham
Adventures of faith
ISBN: 978-1-78259-089-7

Acts 1–12
Church on the move
ISBN: 978-1-85345-574-2

Acts 13–28
To the ends of the earth
ISBN: 978-1-85345-592-6

Barnabas
Son of encouragement
ISBN: 978-1-85345-911-5

Bible Genres
Hearing what the Bible really says
ISBN: 978-1-85345-987-0

Daniel
Living boldly for God
ISBN: 978-1-85345-986-3

David
A man after God's own heart
ISBN: 978-1-78259-444-4

Ecclesiastes
Hard questions and
spiritual answers
ISBN: 978-1-85345-371-7

Elijah
A man and his God
ISBN: 978-1-85345-575-9

Elisha
A lesson in faithfulness
ISBN: 978-1-78259-494-9

Ephesians
Claiming your inheritance
ISBN: 978-1-85345-229-1

Esther
For such a time as this
ISBN: 978-1-85345-511-7

Fruit of the Spirit
Growing more like Jesus
ISBN: 978-1-85345-375-5

Galatians
Freedom in Christ
ISBN: 978-1-85345-648-0

God's Rescue Plan
Finding God's fingerprints
on human history
ISBN: 978-1-85345-294-9

Great Prayers of the Bible
Applying them to our lives toda
ISBN: 978-1-85345-253-6

Hebrews
Jesus – simply the best
ISBN: 978-1-85345-337-3

Hosea
The love that never fails
ISBN: 978-1-85345-290-1

Isaiah 1–39
Prophet to the nations
ISBN: 978-1-85345-510-0

Isaiah 40–66
Prophet of restoration
ISBN: 978-1-85345-550-6

James
Faith in action
ISBN: 978-1-85345-293-2

Jeremiah
The passionate prophet
ISBN: 978-1-85345-372-4

John's Gospel
Exploring the seven miraculous signs
ISBN: 978-1-85345-295-6

Joseph
The power of forgiveness and reconciliation
ISBN: 978-1-85345-252-9

Joshua 1–10
Hand in hand with God
ISBN: 978-1-78259-542-7

Judges 1–8
The spiral of faith
ISBN: 978-1-85345-681-7

Judges 9–21
Learning to live God's way
ISBN: 978-1-85345-910-8

Luke
A prescription for living
ISBN: 978-1-78259-270-9

Mark
Life as it is meant to be lived
ISBN: 978-1-85345-233-8

Mary
The mother of Jesus
ISBN: 978-1-78259-402-4

Moses
Face to face with God
ISBN: 978-1-85345-336-6

Names of God
Exploring the depths of God's character
ISBN: 978-1-85345-680-0

Nehemiah
Principles for life
ISBN: 978-1-85345-335-9

Parables
Communicating God on earth
ISBN: 978-1-85345-340-3

Philemon
From slavery to freedom
ISBN: 978-1-85345-453-0

Philippians
Living for the sake of the gospel
ISBN: 978-1-85345-421-9

Prayers of Jesus
Hearing His heartbeat
ISBN: 978-1-85345-647-3

Proverbs
Living a life of wisdom
ISBN: 978-1-85345-373-1

Revelation 1–3
Christ's call to the Church
ISBN: 978-1-85345-461-5

Revelation 4–22
The Lamb wins! Christ's final victory
ISBN: 978-1-85345-411-0

Rivers of Justice
Responding to God's call to righteousness today
ISBN: 978-1-85345-339-7

Ruth
Loving kindness in action
ISBN: 978-1-85345-231-4

The Armour of God
Living in His strength
ISBN: 978-1-78259-583-0

The Beatitudes
Immersed in the grace of Christ
ISBN: 978-1-78259-495-6

The Covenants
God's promises and their relevance today
ISBN: 978-1-85345-255-0

The Creed
Belief in action
ISBN: 978-1-78259-202-0

The Divine Blueprint
God's extraordinary power in ordinary lives
ISBN: 978-1-85345-292-5

The Holy Spirit
Understanding and experiencing Him
ISBN: 978-1-85345-254-3

The Image of God
His attributes and character
ISBN: 978-1-85345-228-4

The Kingdom
Studies from Matthew's Gospel
ISBN: 978-1-85345-251-2

The Letter to the Romans
Good news for everyone
ISBN: 978-1-85345-250-5

The Lord's Prayer
Praying Jesus' way
ISBN: 978-1-85345-460-8

The Prodigal Son
Amazing grace
ISBN: 978-1-85345-412-7

The Second Coming
Living in the light of Jesus' return
ISBN: 978-1-85345-422-6

The Sermon on the Mount
Life within the new covenant
ISBN: 978-1-85345-370-0

Thessalonians
Building Church in changing times
ISBN: 978-1-78259-443-7

The Ten Commandments
Living God's Way
ISBN: 978-1-85345-593-3

The Uniqueness of our Faith
What makes Christianity distinctive?
ISBN: 978-1-85345-232-1

For current prices or to order, visit **www.cwr.org.uk/store**
Available online or from Christian bookshops.

smallGroup central

*All of our small group ideas
and resources in one place*

Online:

www.smallgroupcentral.org.uk
is filled with free video teaching,
tools, articles and a whole host
of ideas.

On the road:

A range of seminars themed for
small groups can be brought to
your local community. Contact us at
hello@smallgroupcentral.org.uk

In print:

Books, study guides and DVDs
covering an extensive list of themes,
Bible books and life issues.

Log on and find out more at:
www.smallgroupcentral.org.uk

Be inspired by God.
Every day.

Cover to Cover Every Day

In-depth study of the Bible, book by book. Part of a five-year series.

Every Day with Jesus

The popular daily Bible reading notes by Selwyn Hughes.

Inspiring Women Every Day

Daily insight and encouragement written by women for women.

Life Every Day

Lively Bible notes, with Jeff Lucas' wit and wisdom.

To order or subscribe, visit **www.cwr.org.uk/store** or call **01252 784700**.
Also available in Christian bookshops.

 Print subscription available

 **Large Print subscription** available

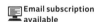 **Email subscription** available

Courses and events

Waverley Abbey College

Publishing and media

Conference facilities

Transforming lives

CWR's vision is to enable people to experience personal transformation through applying God's Word to their lives and relationships.

Our Bible-based training and resources help people around the world to:

- Grow in their walk with God
- Understand and apply Scripture to their lives
- Resource themselves and their church
- Develop pastoral care and counselling skills
- Train for leadership
- Strengthen relationships, marriage and family life and much more.

Our insightful writers provide daily Bible reading notes and other resources for all ages, and our experienced course designers and presenters have gained an international reputation for excellence and effectiveness.

CWR's Training and Conference Centres in Surrey and East Sussex, England, provide excellent facilities in idyllic settings – ideal for both learning and spiritual refreshment.

Applying God's Word
to everyday life and relationships

CWR, Waverley Abbey House,
Waverley Lane, Farnham,
Surrey GU9 8EP, UK

Telephone: **+44 (0)1252 784700**
Email: info@cwr.org.uk
Website: www.cwr.org.uk

Registered Charity No. 294387
Company Registration No. 1990308